Arrows of time

In "Management in New Age: Western Windows Eastern Doors" (1996), Dr. Sharma provides the foundations for a new confluence of Western and Eastern ideas and concepts. The book has been considered 'original and creative' and 'thought provoking' with 'quite a few exciting, non-conventional and revolutionary points of view'.

In "Quantum Rope: Science, Mysticism & Management" (1999), Dr. Sharma combines science, Indian thought and modern management in new perspectives through quantum-rhythmic connections between East and West.

Arrows of Time

from the
Blackholes to the Nirvana Point

Subhash Sharma

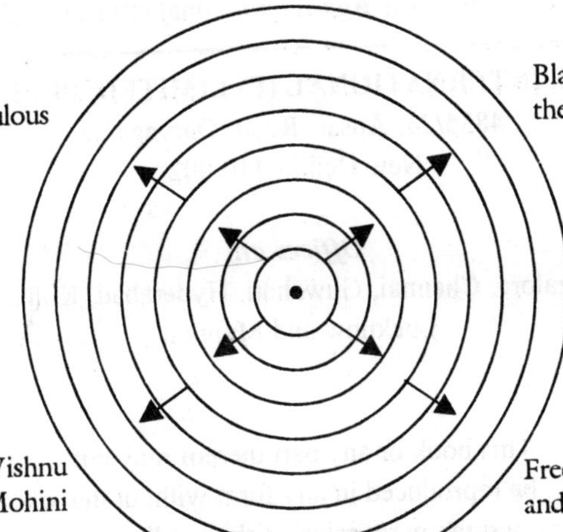

NEW AGE INTERNATIONAL (P) LIMITED, PUBLISHERS
New Delhi • Bangalore • Chennai • Guwahati
Hyderabad • Kolkata • Lucknow • Mumbai

NEW AGE INTERNATIONAL (P) LIMITED, PUBLISHERS
4835/24, Ansari Road, Daryaganj,
New Delhi - 110 002

Offices at:
Bangalore, Chennai, Guwahati, Hyderabad, Kolkata,
Lucknow and Mumbai

ISBN : 81-224-1333-1

Published by K.K. Gupta for New Age International (P) Ltd.,
4835/24, Ansari Road, Daryaganj, New Delhi-110 002 and
printed in India at Saras Graphic, New Delhi - 110 064.

Acknowledgements

Ancient Rishis attained enlightenment under trees. Upanishads were revealed and taught under the trees. Gautaum Buddha attained enlightenment sitting under the tree. A similar story was repeated in a different space time context. Newton sitting under the apple tree had his enlightenment and contributed to strengthening the foundations of science. Spiritual enlightenment and scientific achievements both seem to have the tree connection. During contemporary times also, many including academicians have achieved 'enlightenment' and gained creative insights sitting under a tree of one type or other. The story of writing this book, *Arrows of Time: From Blackholes to Nirvana Point*, also has a tree connection. In 1993, I was waiting for Indian Airlines IC flight from Bombay. The flight was delayed and I used the time to 'meditate' under the tree at the Bangalore airport. There was a feeling of 'enlightenment' whatever that may mean, creating an intuitive flash leading to initial flow of rhythms of the Arrow of Time. The flow continued subsequently and found an expression in an enlarged version of the Arrows of Time. The initial rhythms were published in my book *Quantum Rope: Science, Mysticism & Management*, New Age International Publishers (1999) under the title, "Arrow of Time" (pp.49-56).

This book has been influenced by a large number of sources. It may not be possible for me to identify all of them. The creativity triggers came from many directions leading to some 'revelations', some 'repetitions', some 'reinterpretations' and some 'reinventing'. In particular, Chapter 2 on Space, Time and Consciousness has been influenced by two well-known books, viz. *The Arrow of Time: The Quest to Solve Science's Greatest Mysteries*, Peter Coveney and Roger Highfield (1991) and *The Brief History of Time: From the Big Bang to Blackholes*, Stephen Hawking (1988). In addition, this chapter has also been influenced and enriched by Indian thought.

There are several indigenous influences in the rhythms presented in this book. In particular, influence of Tulsi Ramayana, Kabir dohas, etc. can be observed. Indeed, this work has been influenced by both Western and Eastern ideas, concepts, metaphors and myths. A list of inspirational sources is provided at the end of the book. A few of the poems included in Part - IV were published by the Writers' Forum, Ranchi. These include, "Adam and Eve" (1997), "Circle of Consciousness" (1998), "Point of Light" (1999) and "Lady With a Lamp" (2001). I thank Ravi Nandan Sinha, editor of publications from the Writers' Forum for the permission to include my previously published poems in this book.

What is presented in this book is only a beginning of the journey as the rhythms presented here are unending in nature. In fact, many can join this journey and extend the verses according to their own experiences and orientations. They are welcome to become fellow travellers in time's caravan. I have used the rhythms presented here in creativity and stress management sessions. The experience shows that these rhythms are useful in relieving stress.

In bringing this book to light, I received support from many quarters. While, it may not be possible to individually list the encouragement and support from various sources, I would like to particularly mention the support received from my wife, Krishna Sharma and sons, Munish and Rishikesh, who in many ways participated in this journey. I also thank Ms. T.C.Pushpalatha for her assistance in computer word processing for this book.

Anybody interested in converting this work in any musical form should contact the author.

Subhash Sharma

Bangalore

Contents

Acknowledgements v

1. Introduction xi

2. Space, Time and Consciousness xviii

Part I 1

Scientific Arrow of Time

Arrow of Time (I) ⟶ Blackholes and the Lightholes

Part II 31

Social Arrow of Time

Arrow of Time (II) ⟶ Freedom, Dignity and Liberation

Part III 57

Religious Arrow of Time

Arrow of Time (III) ⟶ Vishnu Came as Mohini

Part IV 69

Spiritual Arrow of Time

Arrow of Time (IV) ⟶ Miraculous

Inspirational Sources 104

1

Introduction

The ideas of matter, space, time and causality have fascinated the human mind since the arrival of humankind on the earth. Before the advent of science people used intuitive metaphors to understand the intricacies of these ideas. Later, scientists provided rigorous definitions and measurement systems to gain better understanding about the space and time. Newton thought in 'Absolute' terms, Einstein made them 'relative' and Quantum physics thought them in terms of 'quantas'. Non-linear dynamics has brought in the terms such as 'chaos' and fuzziness. Eastern thought emphasized the idea of consciousness in perceiving and piercing through the space, time and causality. A combination of all these approaches makes the matter, space, time and causality 'absolutely relative and chaotic quantities' in the form of space-time-consciousness (stc) mosaic wherein space time and consciousness interpenetrate in many non-linear ways giving us a sense about the 'arrow of time'.

This book, *Arrows of Time* is influenced by several paradigms of religion, science and spirituality. Primary inspirational impulse came from the opening verse in Lanka kand in Ramayana which had unconscious and conscious influence in triggering the 'enlightenment' process. This verse is as follows:

> *"O Soul, why do you not worship Rama,*
> *Who has instants, moments, minutes, years, ages and aeons,*
> *For his fierce arrows and Time for his bow".*

Thus, Time is the bow and its arrows are instants, moments, minutes, ages and aeons. As the arrows of time shoot from the bow, they influence events and life's of individuals, societies and all animate and inanimate objects in the universe. At the heart of everything happening around us is the 'Arrow of Time' whose impact we feel in many mysterious ways. Given its importance, Time was elevated to the level of God and has been worshipped in its many forms. Perhaps this is peculiar to India where Time has been referred to as Maha-Kaal. Its worship also has a deeper psycho-analytic and psycho-spiritual meaning as a healing medicine. It may be indicated that in science, the fascinating and evocative term, Arrow of Time was coined by well-known astrophysicist Arthur Eddington in 1927. It is also interesting that in Ramayana we find the idea of time in the form of Rama's 'Bow of Time' and in Mahabharata we find it in the form of Kaal-chakra or the 'Wheel of Time'.

In Gita, Krishna manifests himself as Time. "I am Time, the great destroyer of worlds" (Gita XI, 32). Thus, God is Time and Time is God just as Gandhi's well-known observation that "God is truth and Truth is God". Thus, God as Time and God as Truth lead us to eternal truths of time. Hence, the wheel of time or the kaal-chakra has been an important idea in Indian thought. It may also be indicated that in Indian thought, time has both male and the female forms. Perhaps in no other literature of the world, this dual nature of time has been emphasized. Similarly the four directions are also depicted through the feminine metaphors. These philosophical ideas find their manifestation in various forms in popular culture in the form of poems, songs and other literature. Even Indian cinema has been drawing upon these metaphors of time in various forms. It is merely indicative of all-pervading influence of various philosophical ideas about Space and Time on the collective conscious of the people.

The scientific ideas on arrow of time originated from the need to differentiate between the past, present and future. It is also interesting that in some languages same word is used for the past and future e.g. in Hindi we say "kal aaj aur kal" wherein first 'kal' refers to the past and the second 'kal' refers to the future with present acting as a bridge between the two. In the scientific field, there are many interpretations of arrow of time. In physics, the arrow of time is defined through the law of entropy or the second law of thermodynamics in terms of change from order to disorder. As per the law of entropy, "all things proceed from order to disorder". Past is differentiated from the present by comparing the entropy today with the entropy yesterday. Thus, movement of time is indicated by the change in entropy. In biology, arrow of time is defined in terms of evolution from simple to complex. These two arrows are in opposite directions - a puzzle that fascinates scientists and has yet to be resolved. With the 'quantum arrow of time' moving in all kinds of directions, the past, present and future tend to coalesce in new forms making the time travel in the quantum world a possibility. Like the yogis, man has to transform himself from the sthool or the gross form to sukshma or the subtle form to realize the potentiality of time travel and explore the many-fold parallel universes that co-exist in various space-time zones.

In his treatise, "*A Brief History of Time: From the Big Bang to the Blackholes*," (1988) Stephen Hawking has provided in simple language the complex scientific explanations about the idea of arrow of time. However, the journey from the blackholes to the nirvana point is not in the realm of physics. While Hawking stops at blackholes, Buddha takes us to the nirvana point - explorations of the inner spaces in contrast to explorations of the outer spaces. One deals with the physical world and physical reality out there, the other with the mind world and experiential reality. Both are required for a 'unified' approach to the understanding of the arrow of time and its existential implications.

In this book, I have attempted to understand the meaning of the scientific and experiential ideas related to matter, space, time and causality for our day to day existence. This understanding is expressed in a verse form wherein I have taken the poetic liberty in linking the usefulness of ideas to their practical significance. In the process, ideas from science, religion, spirituality, social sciences, management and other fields are interwoven for adding more meaning to life. It is my hope that through this new blend, we can rediscover the wheel of time and move with it in Buddha's spirit of chairaveti-chairaveti, move on, move on. Idea of blackholes is from physics and the idea of nirvana point is from spirituality. Hence, the subtitle of the book, 'From Blackhole to The Nirvana Point' to indicate the symbiosis of science and spirituality.

This book is divided in four parts broadly around four arrows of time viz. the 'scientific arrow of time', 'social arrow of time', 'religious arrow of time' and the 'spiritual arrow of time'. Hence, each part has a major emphasis. Part-I titled as "Blackholes and Lightholes", largely draws upon scientific ideas and theories related to the ideas on space, time and consciousness. Part-II titled as "Freedom, Dignity and Liberation", explores the arrow of time in terms of day to day existence drawing upon theories, concepts, metaphors from social sciences including management and empirical intelligence of common masses. Hence, we refer to it as 'social arrow of time'. Part-III titled as "Vishnu Came As Mohini" relates the mythological and religious metaphors to the arrow of time. Hence, we refer this section as 'religious arrow of time'. Part-IV titled as "Miraculous" takes us closer to the nirvana point and a feeling of joy and bliss that we experience in dance and music. Accordingly, this part presents the rhythms and rhymes of the arrow of time in its "Miraculous" form through some 'high fever bhajans' and songs capturing the rhythms of wheels of time and motion of the arrows of time emanating from various notes of nature. Hence, we call it as 'spiritual arrow of time'. All the parts complement and supplement each other through symbiosis of religions, science, spirituality and the existential experiences including management of organizations and management of time.

It may be indicated that in writing the *Arrows of Time,* the author has been deeply influenced by at least four 'streams of influences', viz. Sanskrit, Sufi, Subaltern and Science. Sanskrit and Sufi influences manifest in the form of spiritual metaphors. Subaltern influences in the form of existential metaphors. Influence of Science in the form of scientific terms and phrases. Four arrows of time emanating from these four influences move at different speeds in the rhythms presented here. Further, tradition, modern and post-modern ideas have also influenced this work and the metaphors from these three 'streams of thought systems' intermingle in varying forms through a new blend of tradition, modernity and post-modernity.

Evolution of human thought has been unfolding over centuries in the forms of religion, science and spirituality in that order. Religion had deep impact on human thought during ancient times. Subsequently, science influenced the human thinking. Now, spirituality with its emphasis on intuition and creativity is emerging as a new force that is likely to influence the future directions of human thought. 'Science of spirituality' could form a basis for the same. Work of great thinkers such as Vivekananda, Aurobindo and others could form a basis for the same. These three waves overlap each other as can be observed in Fig.1. In several ways these three waves, viz. religion, science and spirituality have influenced this work.

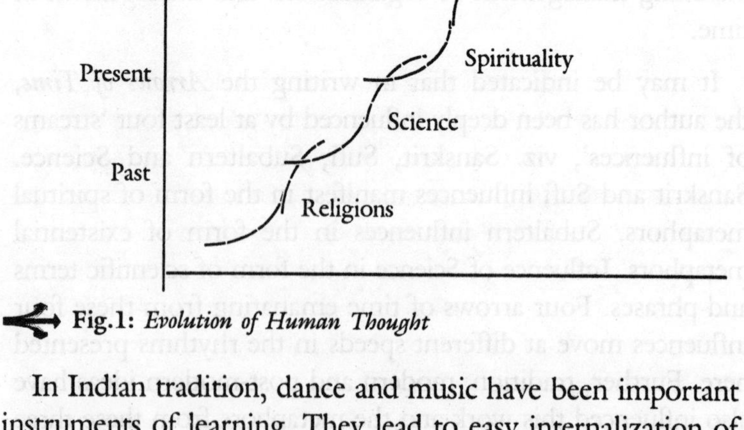

Fig.1: *Evolution of Human Thought*

In Indian tradition, dance and music have been important instruments of learning. They lead to easy internalization of ideas and concepts. My experiments with poetic methodology indicate that this style to learning is not only useful in unlocking creativity in individuals but is also useful in communicating the complex ideas in sublime, subtle and interesting ways. It is my hope that readers of this book may find some literary value in this publication. It may also be useful as a guide for self-reflection and self-transformation. In addition, the book is also useful in teaching social science and management ideas and concepts. It could also be used by management teachers for handling various bows and arrows of time for better time management and social science teachers for enriching their sessions through poetic methodology. My students at several institutes of management, have found this methodology as an enlightening experience. I initially tested the poetic methodology at WISDOM (Women's Institute for Studies in Development Oriented Management), Banasthali, where I found that internalization of management ideas became easy because of the poetic methodology.

In many ways, this book is an extension of my earlier work, *Creation from Shunya* (1993), *Management in New Age: Western Windows Eastern Doors* (1996) and *Quantum Rope: Science, Mysticism & Management* (1999). Hence many ideas, concepts and metaphors discussed in these books, find their echo in one form or the other. The explanatory notes for many ideas and concepts used in *Arrows of Time* are available in above mentioned books. Interested readers may refer to these books and the references provided therein.

2

Space Time and Consciousness

This discussion on Arrow of Time assumes reader's familiarity with most important theories of science. For the Western readers it assumes that they are familiar with Indian mythological insights to the ideas of space, time, evolution, involution and maya or 'illusion' etc.

The concept of time has been with us since time immemorial. In Indian philosophy and folklore at least three distinct ideas exist about the nature of time. Time as Kaal-chakra or wheel, is indicative of the rhythmic nature of time. From the micro wheels to the macro wheels of the yugas, time shows its ritam or the rhythm in the biological clocks, chemical clocks and the cosmic clocks. The second idea of time as Rama's bow is close to the modern metaphor of the arrow of time. The third idea of time as Brahma's day having equivalence to 43,20,000,000 years on earth reminds us of the relativity ratio of 1:43,20,000,000 in the cosmological sense. In addition to these ideas about time, emergence, end and re-emergence of time is also metaphorically described in various ways. The trinity of Brahama, Vishnu and Mahesh describes the process of creation, evolution and dissolution of the world in terms of its matter, space, time and cosmic consciousness. These ideas about the 'arrows of time' also find expression in popular consciousness in terms of poetic expositions of saints and sages of India.

Scientific studies about the nature of time and time processes in terms of arrow of time are relatively of recent origin. Though the clocks to measure the time are quite old, the expression 'arrow of time' is of recent origin in science. Various 'paradigms' of science have added new dimensions to this idea. As a result, many contradictions in scientific theories have also come to light. Indeed several theories that were considered as 'final' theories to understand matter, space and time have been found to be applicable only within certain ranges or levels of reality.

Science is now coming closer to the observation that there are various levels of reality and different theories explain different reality only at one level or the other. Thus, Newton's laws of motion are applicable only within a range. Newton's laws of motion break down "to describe the very fast, very massive and the very small". At the microscopic level, quantum theory emerged as a new theory to explain the 'laws of nature' in the 'zoo of particles'. At the speed of light, Einstein theory changed the notion of absolute space and time to relative view of space and time. Thus, a theory that was considered as an ultimate triumph of science over religion at one point of time turned out to be only a partial theory.

Newton's laws of motion are time symmetric. Thus, there is no distinction between past and future. Further, causality and determinism are at the heart of Newton's laws and worldviews. Given initial conditions and data, the rest was merely a matter of calculations through the Newton's equations. So strong was the faith in these laws at one point of time, that any alternative view was hearsay. Only a new revolution in science could change this faith. This new revolution was brought by Einstein through his theory of relativity. Thus, the notions of absolute space and time in which there was an absolute faith before Einstein changed. Einstein gave a new interpretation to gravity in terms of space-time curvatures due to presence of mass. Einstein's theory became a new faith. But the world turned out to be having beauty spots of blackholes and space-time shortcuts of wormholes, representing the singularities where the laws of physics fail. Relativity theory had its failure at the level of the quantum world. It was also deterministic in nature but the quantum world turned out to be full of uncertainties and probabilities. "God does not play dice" is a famous quote of Einstein, but Krishna plays dice in its literal sense as we know from the Mahabharata. Thus, Einstein could not reconcile to the 'theories' of the quantum world, though he got his noble prize for his contribution on photoelectric effect, which was a contribution to the quantum theory. Thus, we find at least, three paradigms of science viz. Newtonian, Einsteinian and the quantum physics each valid in its own range with its own geometry.

The story of physics does not end with these three paradigms of science or the three forms of geometry in the form of Euclidean, Reimmanian and fractal. There is another interesting law viz. the second law of thermodynamics, which explains the nature of entropy. Also known as law of increase of entropy, it suggests that there is an increase in disorder. As a consequence of increase in entropy, one day the world will reach a point of heat-death, a metaphor similar to the pralaya concept. Second law of thermodynamics gives an explicit recognition to the arrow of time that moves from the past to the future indicated by the increase in entropy.

It may be useful to point out a similarity between the idea of entropy in the second law of thermodynamics and the idea of adharma in Indian thought. There is also an interesting parallel of the second law of thermodynamics with the Indian idea of yugas—Satyuga, Dwapar, Treta and Kaliyuga, wherein there is an increase in adharma or entropy. The cycle of yugas is indicative of the increasing social entropy and when the cycle is completed there is re-emergence of satyuga. Thus, both the ideas viz. the cyclical and forward movement of the arrow of time are inherent in this concept. While, the second law of thermodynamics leads us to heat death and provides no explanation for the start of the new cycle, the yuga concept is indicative of the movement from order to disorder but goes beyond it and indicates the start of a new order after the disorder. The second law of thermodynamics is a 'blind' law of nature as it merely describes the phenomenon of entropy. The theory of yugas indicates that as the kaliyuga runs its course, the conditions are set for the arrival of the Krishna like person or the avatara to make the change in the direction of a new order out of chaos. In a way, the wheel of time is reversed through a 'divine intervention' or a mysterious law of nature! There is an interesting sloka in Gita to highlight this idea:

> *"Whenever there is decline of order and disorder shows its rise,*
> *O Bharata in such situations I myself arise".*

Second law of thermodynamics has troubled many scientists. It is consistent with the idea of arrow of time. It views the world in terms of changes from the order to disorder with increases in entropy. It suggests heat death -

far into future. However, this arrow of time is in opposition to another arrow of time reflected in the theory of evolution, which suggests evolution of life from simplicity to complexity, from 'lower' forms to 'higher' forms. Thus, we have two curves of nature, one rising curve described by theory of evolution where there is a rise from the lower order to higher order and the other falling curve where there is decline in order leading to rise in disorder. Hence, a question arises with respect to the limits of these laws or the specific situations in which these laws are valid. A universal theory eliminating the contradictions between these laws is yet to be formulated. Perhaps just like the wave particle duality, nature shows its contradictions. On the one hand there is increase in entropy on the other there is increase in order. In its inanimate form, nature behaves according to second law of thermodynamics and in its animate form it longs for evolution. Nature in its 'dead' form follows the second law of thermodynamics and in its live form it shows its urge for evolution.

It may be indicated that an equivalent of the evolution theory is also available in Indian mythology in the form of dasavatara. This concept also indicates the evolution of the higher forms of life from the lower forms. Indian dasavatara theory is also indicative of the 'evolution of consciousness' and not merely 'evolution of matter'. The idea of Kalki avatara is indicative of the direction of evolution towards a 'cosmic civilization'. Thus, in Indian mythology also we have two approaches, one indicating the increase in disorder through the motion of yugas and the other indicating the increase in order through the higher forms of life. However, the two get reconciled through the arrival of avatara i.e. some form of human intervention to create a change from disorder to order by reversing the entropy. Order-disorder and new order represents the essence of this dynamics. When order and chaos interact, a new order emerges and a new cycle of this interaction begins. This is the crux of the change theory. Similar idea is also indicated by action-reaction and interaction concept as well as Hegel's idea of thesis-antithesis and synthesis. However, when order and chaos interact there are interesting feedback processes and 'self-organizing' tendencies in nature which could lead to unpredictable new order. This indicates that there is no determinism in the order-disorder interaction.

In the realm of science, efforts to make a bridge between the second law of thermodynamics and Darwin's theory of evolution have lead to new ideas and perspectives. The effort is to show, "how creatures like man, containing structures of exquisite sophistication, might emerge in a universe where entropy is increasing" (Coveney & Highfield, 1991, p.36). It is increasingly being realized that nature is not a set of linear equations. It has many non-linear features which manifest in nature's functioning in many ways. Non-linearity also implies, "getting more than what you bargained for". There is plenty of free lunch provided, you know how to get it! There are many, who are masters of this art. Theory of chaos is rooted in the non-linear equations and topological interpretations of the world around us. Nature shows self-organizing tendencies and is rich in feedback processes, both the positive feedback and the negative feedback. It throws up new patterns in situations that are far from equilibrium. Thus, novelty through new and unpredictable phase space is inherent in nature. While on the one hand entropy is increasing, on the other there is self-organization, there is novelty, hence, the possibility of man emerging from the 'lower forms'. Thus, nature simultaneously displays disorder and order tendencies. This duality is a part of nature.

If man has evolved from lower order life forms as the evolution theory and dasavatara mythology indicate, can man also go through the reverse process? While current science may reject this proposition but a clue for the same exists in 'mythology' or religion. According to rebirth hypothesis, life form can get manifested itself in millions of ways which could be the 'lower order' life forms. This belief is typical to the Indian subcontinent but provides a clue to the higher order mysteries of nature. According to this belief, man may jump down several steps of the evolutionary ladder depending upon the result of 'accumulated actions' or the karma. Whether we believe in this proposition or not, it provides us an interesting thought experiment about a 'parallel' world, wherein there is descent from higher form of life to lower form of life. Perhaps both evolution and descent are part of nature, one operating in this world the other in a parallel world. May be evolution is not irreversible phenomenon, but a reversible one and there are many paths to reversibility represented by many life forms. In fact, the idea of rebirth is as fascinating as the idea of time travel. Time travel looks impossible to the humans because arrow of time moves from the past to the future. It is unidirectional. Similarly rebirth looks impossible perhaps because of restrictive understanding about involution of life into different patterns. If there is 'survival of consciousness', then consciousness can reappear in different patterns and forms and rebirth may be possible in this physical world just like the possibility of time travel in science fiction.

It may be indicated that Stephen Hawking (1988) identifies at least three arrows of time viz. the thermodynamic arrow of time, psychological arrow of time and the cosmological arrow of time. Increase in entropy defines the thermodynamic arrow of time. As human beings we feel the passing of time from past to present to future. This psychological arrow of time represents the 'direction of time in which we remember the past and not the future'. The third is the cosmological arrow of time representing the 'direction of time in which the universe is expanding rather than contracting'. Indeed the fascinating field of cosmology provides a testing ground for many theories of physics. Process of creation, evolution and destruction was initially represented in a trinity form viz. Brahama, Vishnu and Mahesh. The ideas of creation, expansion and involution are also part of this 'mythological' approach to cosmology. After the pralaya or dissolution, the world retraces itself in a new creation. Thus, a continuous creation and destruction is envisaged and new cycles of time begin. While these mythological interpretations still fascinate human beings, science has also been grappling with the issues of creation, evolution and dissolution of the world through the ideas of 'big bang' and 'big crunch'. There is lot of speculation in this field of science and several theories float around. These include the big bang, expanding universe, the steady state, the big crunch etc. Interestingly some of these theories are coming closer to the Eastern mythological views about the creation of universe. In any case the parallels seem to be interesting. Consider the following Hymn of creation from Rigveda translated by Swami Vivekananda:

"Existence was not then, nor non-existence,
The world was not, the sky beyond was neither,
What covered the mist? Of whom was that?
What was in the depth of darkness thick?

Death was not then, nor immortality,
The night was neither separate from day,
But motionless did that vibrate,
Alone, with its own glory one,
Beyond that nothing did exist,

At first in darkness hidden darkness lay,
Undistinguished as one mass of water,
That which lay in void thus covered,
A glory did put forth by Tapah!"

It was initially believed that cosmological events could be explained completely through Newton's formulations. However, Einstein introduced new concepts of cosmological curvatures and time dilations. While Einstein's ideas were an improvement over Newton, they were also rooted in the deterministic view of the world. With the ideas of blackholes, wormholes and baby universes, new dimensions have been added to cosmological complexities. Indeed, the search for the cosmological arrow of time is still on. What it implies is that new theories may emerge in future that would provide better explanation of the world around us. Till that time the journey of science must continue.

We have taken an overview of various paradigms of science, their contradictions and multiple interpretations to the way we view the world. We have not so far introduced the notion of consciousness. The idea of consciousness is entering the field of science from two routes viz. via the route of artificial intelligence and the route of Eastern mysticism. The former is still the 'matter' route to consciousness, the latter is 'spiritual' route to consciousness. Thus, 'body', 'mind' and 'spirit' are entering the realm of science through the 'matter', 'mind' ('intelligence') and consciousness ('cosmic intelligence'). Merger of science and spirituality seems to be the future direction of science itself. Thus, 'lower order' science may evolve into 'higher order' science. The laws of lower order science manifested in its ideas of space-time and causality may continue to exist along with the laws of higher order science wherein the notions of space-time and causality acquire new meanings. This does not mean complete rejection of the lower order science. It only implies a better understanding of its limitations.

In the notion of stc - space time consciousness, dimensions of space, time and consciousness interpenetrate. Space and time are merely projections of human mind. Maya or the 'illusion' is at its root. Perhaps, the world around us is both a real world as well as maya. In the real world the arrow of time moves from the lower entropy to higher entropy. As we transcend these real worlds and reach the 'parallel' world, the laws of physics break down and the laws of spiritual dynamics take over, where there is no space time and causation as we understand from the laws of physics. Perhaps mystics can travel across these two world with ease and that is why they consider even this world as maya. They can reverse the arrow of time and feel the pulse of the world where 'Ganga flows from the ocean to the Himalaya', 'Where anything can be created from nothing', 'Where bull exits from the China shop after keeping everything in order', 'Where broken pieces of a cup automatically get combined to form a cup', 'Where apples rise from the ground and get attached to the tree for a reverse process', 'Where apples don't fall on Newton's head', etc. etc. Such a place would be full of adventure and most people would be interested in taking a journey of such a place before their death. It is believed that near death experiences do lead a credence to such adventurous places where arrow of time moves in reverse direction. Indeed such space-time zones could co-exist with the real world. Time could be 'linear' at one level, 'curved' at another level and 'fractal' at yet another level of existence. In a 'view from the consciousness', physical world and the space time could merely be a projection from a parallel world to a physical world. In this process of projection everything gets into proper shape. Ganga flows from Himalaya to the oceans, though in 'reality' it may be happening the other way round. The 'collapse of the wave functions' at the inter-crossings of the physical world and the 'parallel' world, may be creating the mirror image of the original event, which we experience in the physical world.

While blackholes and wormholes could provide us short cuts to various universes just like Narada used to appear and disappear, the nirvana point can take us to the world where arrow of time is running backward and 'river of time' is flowing from other Universes. It could as well be the point of cross section between the physical world and the 'parallel world' where arrow of time runs from past to future to the world of the Shangri La where arrow of time could move in various directions. Hence, the sub title of this book, "From the Blackholes to the Nirvana Point".

Part I

Scientific Arrow of Time

Blackholes and the Lightholes
1(1) - 1(84)

Arrow of Time

(I)

Time moves on and on
It doesn't wait
There is change of date
But time doesn't wait
Yesterday, today, tomorrow
Are part of time's arrow
This arrow moves on and on
It doesn't wait
Time moves on and on
It doesn't wait. 1(1)

We wait at time's gate
But time doesn't wait
It moves at snail's pace
It goes at fast rate
It may stand standstill
But it doesn't wait
Time moves on and on
It doesn't wait. 1(2)

Some times it is fast
Some times it is slow
Relativity is part of its continuous flow
It flows on and on
It doesn't wait
Time moves on and on
It doesn't wait. 1(3)

You indulge in passing the time
Time surpasses you
Its history is written
On every particle of dew
It encompasses in itself
Both old and new
Time moves on and on
It doesn't wait. 1(4)

We want to communicate
With time's various dates
It hides in its flow
Our destiny and our fate
Time moves on and on
It doesn't wait. 1(5)

Clocks may stop
But time doesn't stop
It does not care
For the orders of the Pope
Moving in the circles
It moves forward and backward
Going through the cycles

It speaks its own Word
Time moves on and on
It doesn't wait. 1(6)

As we enter time's sphere
Time speeds up
We then reach the future's tunnel
Passing through time's funnel
Time moves on and on
Taking us through the tunnels
Time moves on and on
It doesn't wait. 1(7)

When we open time box
We see a black box
Black box contains in itself
Black boards of the self
Containing information of previous births
Also telling us the story of this earth
Time moves on and on
It doesn't wait. 1(8)

Evolution and revolution
Lie on time's path
With movement of the shuttle
They weave time's cloth
Like Draupadi's sari
It doesn't stop
Time moves on and on
It doesn't wait. 1(9)

Matter and energy play a dance
In the time and space
Many universes take a chance
In the superspace
Purusha and prakriti are engaged
In their interplay
Unmanifest becomes manifest
In its unique way
Time moves on and on
It doesn't wait. 1(10)

Time, motion and distance
Position, momentum and their sense
Past, present and future tense
On each other they are leaning
And acquire a new meaning
New ideas come on and on
They don't stop
Time moves on and on
It doesn't wait. 1(11)

Mass becomes energy
Energy becomes mass
There is change of character
In ideas of every class
Change goes on and on
It doesn't stop
Time moves on and on
It doesn't wait. 1(12)

In between two points
There is always infinity
We travel through the time
And reach a new city
We then say neti, neti
Time becomes pretty
Time moves on and on
Like footprints of the Yeti
Time moves on and on
It doesn't wait. 1(13)

As we become fully photon
Photos move on and on
In space time frame they are frozen
But emerge to walk on and on
Statues become alive
And continue their drive
Time moves on and on
It doesn't wait. 1(14)

In the grand space-time world
Gravity makes lines curved
We then take a quantum jump
And reach a parallel world
This world is fascinating
To it we start relating
And time moves on and on
It doesn't wait. 1(15)

Wherever matter is present
Space-time gets distorted
Leading to creation of holes

In which we get jolted
We cross the connecting bridge
And reach the other ridge
Where time is moving backward
We see the Adam's rib
Time moves on and on
It doesn't wait. 1(16)

Every fall of the apple
Is heard in gravity's temple
Like the steps of a drunkard
This world becomes a gamble
This gambling goes on and on
It doesn't stop
Time moves on and on
It doesn't wait. 1(17)

As we look from time's window
We see time and its shadow
We feel the motion of time's arrow
In the flutters of the sparrow
Time's fluttering goes on and on
It doesn't stop
Time moves on and on
It doesn't wait. 1(18)

When we see through time's vision
We see new cosmic regions
Through the window we see horizon
We see fission and fusion
Fission and fusion go on and on
They don't stop

Time moves on and on
It doesn't wait. 1(19)

As we move on space-time triangle
Time shows its angles
Like the music of the bangles
In time's music we get entangled
Time's music goes on and on
It doesn't stop
Time moves on and on
It doesn't wait. 1(20)

We extend our sensors
Through the time's tensors
There are efforts of censure
To force us to say yes Sir
But rebels go on and on
They don't wait
Time moves on and on
It doesn't wait. 1(21)

As the arrow becomes dynamic
It reveals the thermo-dynamic
When it gives us subjective sense
Many decry it as non-sense
Many wonder at its tricks
Time's tricks go on and on
They don't stop
Time moves on and on
It doesn't wait. 1(22)

Kaun-tvam, who are you
This is a quantum question
Scientists and mystics seek answers
And give their new narrations
As they meet the time
At the life-death junction
They describe soul's journey
Through various space-time stations
Time moves on and on
Showing unique relations
Time moves on and on
It doesn't wait. 1(23)

Tick, tick, tick, tick
Time's pendulum
And the beating
Of the drum
As quantum jumps make us Gautum
We gather a new momentum
Time moves on and on
It doesn't wait. 1(24)

Direction of arrow we want to know
In the chamber of neutrino
We then say, no, no, no, no
Where is the music of Piano
Arrow moves in all directions
It doesn't wait
Time moves on and on
It doesn't wait. 1(25)

Cause effect geometry
Has many ridges
They are inter-connected
Through time's hanging bridges
As we speed up
Through the time's path
Curious turns take us
To time's new warps
These turns are very sharp
And show their unique arc
Time move on and on
It doesn't wait. 1(26)

In just few minutes
We see many million years
We witness in few moments
Time's different layers
This very moment contains
Time's previous history
It also fully retains
Time's future story
Time moves on and on
It doesn't wait. 1(27)

Past becomes future
Future becomes past
Past, present and future
Acquire a new cast
This casting goes on and on
It doesn't wait
Time moves on and on
It doesn't wait. 1(28)

Our voice is recorded
On the time's tape
We listen to it
In its various shapes
We whither into time
But tape moves on
Time moves on and on
It doesn't wait. 1(29)

A moment appears near
Then it becomes far
Moments show their twinkle
Like the little star
This twinkling goes on and on
It doesn't stop
Time moves on and on
It doesn't wait. 1(30)

Nature shows its geometry
In symmetry and non symmetry
We search for super-symmetry
In history, physics and chemistry
This search goes on and on
It doesn't stop
Time moves on and on
It doesn't wait. 1(31)

We hop, skip and jump
To look back at the jumps
Into future we jump
And wonder at time's bumps
Time moves on and on

Taking its own jumps
Time moves on and on
It doesn't wait. 1(32)

Time tapestry is woven
By various space-time threads
Moments may be frozen
But time moves ahead
As it takes turns
Which are very sharp
We may get locked in
In the time's warp
Time moves on and on
It doesn't wait. 1(33)

Time tells us
It is time for change
As we communicate
Through the time exchange
Time moves on and on
Bringing in the change
As we look at the time
And its wide range
Time moves on and on
It doesn't wait. 1(34)

We see and feel in nature
The simple harmonic motion
Matter shows vibrations
As if they were chosen
We create a periodic table

Periods show their fables
Time's periods go on and on
They don't stop
Time moves on and on
It doesn't wait. 1(35)

Through the raga we send vibrations
Which then hit the clouds
There is merging of quantum waves
Which brings the rains down
Time's vibrations move into future
Bringing its rains now
Time moves on and on
It doesn't wait. 1(36)

Sun and moon continue their motion
In the time's flow
Billions of stars beautify the sky
In the cosmic show
Time's show goes on and on
It doesn't wait
Time moves on and on
It doesn't wait. 1(37)

Time moves on its feet
Leaving its prints behind
These prints create an impact
On the consciousness and on mind
Time's printing goes on and on
it doesn't stop
Time moves on and on
It doesn't wait. 1(38)

Space is static, time moves on
Time becomes static, space shows its forms
Like the oceanic waves
Space and time show their raves
They move together
Like wrinkes on the leather
Space-time wrinkling goes on and on
It doesn't stop
Time moves on and on
It doesn't wait. 1(39)

We ride on the time's waves
To cross the time's sea
As we reach the other shore
Many time waves we see
The waves move on and on
They do not wait
Time moves on and on
It doesn't wait. 1(40)

Time's arrow is the Mahakaal
Taking us through rise and fall
From the fall a river arises
Making many creations noises
Time's noises go on and on
They don't stop
And time moves on and on
It doesn't wait. 1(41)

In waking state we live in past
Which is a basis for reason
In dreaming state we live in future

Which is the basis for intuition
Past, future, reason and intuition
Affect the present situation
Present moves on and on
It doesn't stop
Time moves on and on
It doesn't wait. 1(42)

Horizontal, vertical and radial
Virtual, imaginary and the real
In many ways mind shows its imagination
To understand creator and the creation
Imaginations go on and on
They don't stop
Time moves on and on
It doesn't wait. 1(43)

Cypher space is hanging
On the time's thread
Time's merrygo moves
In the cosmic shed
This world then arises
From our own head
And reveals to everyone
Its wide spread
Time's merrygo goes round and round
It doesn't stop
Time moves on and on
It doesn't wait. 1(44)

Time becomes space
Space becomes time
Space-time then reveals its unique rhyme
This rhyme shows its curls
Like the surface of the pearl
It continues to curl
Moving like long hairs of a girl
Time's curling goes on and on
It doesn't wait
Time moves on and on
It doesn't wait. 1(45)

Space and time are two leaves
And space-time is a bud
Under gravity they interweave
And the bud opens with a thud
This world becomes a flower
Under the gravity's shower
This shower goes on and on
It doesn't wait
Time moves on and on
It doesn't wait. 1(46)

With one leg in the space
And another one in time
We take a walk across
Through corridors of space and time
And in just three steps
We take a cosmic trek
This trekking goes on and on
It doesn't stop.

Time moves on and on
It doesn't wait. 1(47)

In between two seconds
There is a vast distance
Travelled by the light
And seen by second's lense
We can travel it
At the light's instance
And experience dilation of time
In the light's presence
The seconds move on and on
Covering the cosmic distance
Time moves on and on
It doesn't wait. 1(48)

We look into space-time mirrors
We see many figures
They exist along with us
In universes far and near
Our duplicate comes to us
To say us hello dear
Like Narada he brings happiness
And also lot of cheers
Time moves on and on
Bringing tears and cheers
Time moves on and on
It doesn't wait. 1(49)

In the space-time we are born
In the space-time we cry
We move like photon

And find it maya's lie
Time moves on and on
Without feeling shy
Time moves on and on
It doesn't wait. 1(50)

Space-time shows its twist
And in space-time we exist
We then fully disappear
In the space-time mist
Time moves on and on
Showing its own geist
Time moves on and on
It doesn't wait. 1(51)

We are connected with soul
Which dwells in parallel universe
It moves freely in space and time
And brings for us a new verse
Time moves on and on
Bringing its own verse
Time moves on and on
It doesn't wait. 1(52)

With backward motion of time
We reach past through worldlines
Lines are crossing other lines
World events then get intertwined
We see the events still happening
Future's incoming and going
Time's motion goes on and on
It doesn't stop.

Time moves on and on
It doesn't wait. 1(53)

You throw a stone into pond
There are many ripples
From the centre time begins
And moves with the ripples
As ripples move back in time
We feel the time's shrill
Time's shrilling go on and on
It doesn't stop
Time moves on and on
It doesn't wait. 1(54)

Twins move to different planets
And see the happenings on earth
Each takes a relative view
Under the time's girth
Twin experiences go on and on
Making things relative
Time moves on and on
It doesn't wait. 1(55)

As we move on space-time string
In our ears a new geometry rings
We go in search of time's holy grail
Time leaves behind its holi trails
Time's holi goes on and on
It doesn't stop
Time moves on and on
It doesn't wait. 1(56)

As we speed through time's fly over
Some new places we discover
Are we in the past or future
Or like Trishanku midway in the air
Discoveries go on and on
They don't stop
Time moves on and on
It doesn't wait. 1(57)

We want to log in
To read the time chip
We miss the pass word
In the time's slip
Chip gets updated
As time moves on
Time moves on and on
It doesn't wait. 1(58)

As time performs tandava dance
We feel the impact of quantum chance
Particles display their charm
In particle zoo, there is romance
This romance goes on and on
It doesn't wait
Time moves on and on
It doesn't wait. 1(59)

We now sing the time's song
Which moves like the ping-pong
When we miss a few shots
We see the time and its knots

Time's ping-pong goes on and on
It doesn't wait
Time moves on and on
It doesn't wait. 1(60)

Many branches of the time's tree
With time's wind they float free
Time's leaves move in all directions
In various space-time zones
Their movement goes on and on
It doesn't wait
Time moves on and on
It doesn't wait. 1(61)

We visit the time's temple
Time says, welcome welcome
It is time for inner peace
To cut the ego into piece
Ego's plays go on and on
It doesn't wait
Time moves on and on
It doesn't wait. 1(62)

As we speed up on time's freeway
We see its beauty on the way
We want to have our own say
As the time swings and sway
Time's swinging goes on and on
It doesn't stop
Time moves on and on
It doesn't wait. 1(63)

When we drive on space-time street
There is change in hours and feet
We are moving in relative motion
On the street we find some commotion
Our drive goes on and on
Criss-crossing new streets
Time moves on and on
Along with us on the streets
Time moves on and on
It doesn't wait. 1(64)

After travelling in time's train
Now we board time's plane
We fly through many space-time lanes
And discover future and its many chains
Time's flight goes on and on
It doesn't wait
Time moves on and on
It doesn't wait. 1(65)

When we enter time machine
We then see many new scenes
Scenes of future and of past
In time's mould they are cast
Time's machine moves on and on
It doesn't wait
Time moves on and on
It doesn't wait. 1(66)

Mind itself is a time machine
Taking us to places seen and unseen
From the future it brings information

And reveals to us many new formations
Time's bits flow on and on
They don't wait
Time moves on and on
It doesn't wait. 1(67)

As we become a point of light
And move in space-time spiral
We experience many dimensions
And also time's reversal
On a large computer screen
We move like the cursor
Time's cursor moves on and on
It doesn't wait
Time moves on and on
It doesn't wait. 1(68)

Quantum waves, ghosts or spirits
Call them whatever name
They are nature's hidden mysteries
Showing their unique game
This game goes on and on
It doesn't wait
Time moves on and on
It doesn't wait. 1(69)

In dreams we move at high velocity
And reach new space-time scenes
We find universes overlapping
Curled up like the beans
From the future to the past
We move without obstruction

Time's dream goes on and on
Giving its own instructions
Time moves on and on
It doesn't wait. 1(70)

Space is warp and time is weft
Their weaving creates space-time set
There are tensions in this set
Created by knots in the net
Time's weaving goes on and on
It doesn't stop
Time moves on and on
It doesn't wait. 1(71)

We move along space-time curvature
In our sleep, and in leisure
We beam up with beam of laser
And measure the measures of curvature
Time's beaming goes on and on
It doesn't stop
Time moves on and on
It doesn't wait. 1(72)

Even if we are not there
Apples will continue falling
Of course we will not hear
The sound of air roaring
Time's roaring goes on and on
It doesn't wait
Time moves on and on
It doesn't wait. 1(73)

As we are enamoured by the past
We see the Jurassic park
Scientists search for the quarks
And children see the sparks
To the past we are relating
For the future we are waiting
This waiting goes on and on
It doesn't stop
Time moves on and on
It doesn't wait. 1(74)

An event happens on this earth
Through the light it travels
It then reaches other planets
And is seen in its vision set
On the earth it is seen as past
On the planet it becomes present
From the past to the present
A message is being sent
Your past and my present
Are witnessed by the crescent
Time witnessing goes on and on
It doesn't stop
Time moves on and on
It doesn't wait. 1(75)

Minutes and hours, where do they go
They merge with space like Cupid's arrow
Mystic and scientists want to know
Motion of space-time and its arrow
This arrow moves on and on

It doesn't stop
Time moves on and on
It doesn't wait. 1(76)

We leave behind the time's path
And chart out a new walk
We stop and listen to time's talk
And write it with time's chalk
Time's writing goes on and on
It doesn't stop
Time moves on and on
It doesn't wait. 1(77)

We think of imaginary space
And of imaginary time
In our imaginary geometry
There is an imaginary line
This space-time line goes on and on
It doesn't stop
Time moves on and on
It doesn't wait. 1(78)

We see the earth from cosmic distance
It glows as a point of light
In the cosmic ocean of stars
This point is a beautiful sight
Points move on and on
In the cosmic sea
Time moves on and on
It doesn't wait. 1(79)

In the arrow's reversal
There is a great rehearsal
Broken pieces get combined
To give life a new shine
New creations go on and on
They don't stop
Time moves on and on
It doesn't wait. 1(80)

We aim a ball on snooker's table
And hit it by a cue
Balls are then no more stable
Unpredictable is their move
Time's snooker game goes on and on
It doesn't stop
Time moves on and on
It doesn't wait. 1(81)

We feel the depth of time
In the cyber space
Time then curls up
Around the time's vase
Time's curling goes on and on
It doesn't wait
Time moves on and on
It doesn't wait. 1(82)

Stimulus and response create a cycle
Which is unpredictable
We search for determinism
But uncertainty takes over
Unpredictability becomes a law

Some call it nature's flaw
But this law shows its order
Even in disorder
God plays the dice
Once, twice and thrice
God's play goes on and on
It doesn't' stop
Time moves on and on
It doesn't wait. 1(83)

A bottle is thrown in the sea
You want to know
Where it will be
Its position is surely uncertain
It is difficult to predict its terrain
Bottle moves on and on
From one shore to another
Time move on and on
It doesn't wait. 1(84)

Part II

Social Arrow of Time

Freedom, Dignity and Liberation
2(1) - 2(72)

Arrow of Time

(II)

Time's ladder takes us up
And snakes take us down
Up and down, up and down
We move in time's town
This up and down goes on and on
It doesn't stop
Time moves on and on
It doesn't wait. 2(1)

With the time we move ahead
With the time we grow
With the time we fall down
And with the time we slow
With the time we glow
And with the time we flow
Time moves on and on
And continues to flow
Time moves on and on
It doesn't wait. 2(2)

We measure the money's growth
With time's measuring rod
There is plentifulness
And there are empty pots
Time's measurement goes on and on
It doesn't stop
Time moves on and on
It doesn't wait. 2(3)

Space, time and money
Their relationship is funny
When space and time collapse in money
Time goes for running
Time's running goes on and on
It doesn't stop
Time moves on and on
It doesn't wait. 2(4)

Time moves fast
In the market place
On the sea beach
It moves at its pace
In the market place
Time becomes money
In the cosmic space
Time has a new meaning
Time's dilation goes on and on
It doesn't stop
Time moves on and on
It doesn't wait. 2(5)

Risk, return and peace of mind
Money and power make some blind
Time continues its grind
In time's treasure, new things we find
Time's grinding goes on and on
It doesn't stop
Time moves on and on
It doesn't wait. 2(6)

Globalization is brought to your door
By a writ and an order
This order creates a disorder
In the social border
Disorder goes on and on
It doesn't stop
Time moves on and on
It doesn't wait. 2(7)

Be prepared for the loss
In order to make a gain
Both in the cross and the loss
There is pleasure and pain
Loss and gain go on and on
It doesn't wait
Time moves on and on
It doesn't wait. 2(8)

Saris are produced in Chanderi
They are then sold in Andheri
Profits are made by merchants
In producers' condition, no improvement

This exploitation goes on and on
It doesn't stop
Time moves on and on
It doesn't wait. 2(9)

With the rise of capital
There is fall in water table
With increase in exploitation
There is fall of civilisation
Rise and fall go on and on
At the same time
Time moves on and on
It doesn't wait. 2(10)

Koo-hoo koo-hoo of the Koel
Nice smell of the soil
Lamps create light from oil
Profits come from labour's toil
This toiling goes on and on
It doesn't stop
Time moves on and on
It doesn't wait. 2(11)

Time encircles itself
Like the serpent's coil
It gets unfolded
In the farmer's soil
As the plough moves on and on
There is turning of time's foil
Time moves on and on
It doesn't wait. 2(12)

From revelation comes revolution
This is a basic lesson
In between the two
There are inter-connections
Revelations create new momentum
History shows its motion
Revolutions move on and on
They don't stop
Time moves on and on
It doesn't wait. 2(13)

Tradition and modernity
Make their moves
In order to touch the future
As both become a story
And get lost in time's glory
Then new traditions arrive
On the time' screen
Time moves on and on
It doesn't wait. 2(14)

Position, opposition and proposition
Create new situations
There is conflict and co-operation
In the time's many relations
Propositions go on and on
They don't stop
Time moves on and on
It doesn't wait. 2(15)

Thesis and anti-thesis
Create a new synthesis
With action and reaction
We move towards interaction
This process goes on and on
It doesn't wait
Time moves on and on
It doesn't wait. 2(16)

Point and anti-point
Balance the power equation
Matter and anti-matter
Explode in annihilation
Time's explosions go on and on
They don't stop
Time moves on and on
It doesn't wait. 2(17)

Is it survival of the fittest
Or arrival of the best
For the survival of the weakest
And protection of our nest
In the future time will tell
What is hidden in nature's chest
Time moves on and on
Making its own conquest
Time moves on and on
It doesn't wait. 2(18)

With the fall of the fittest
Things take new shape
There is change of taste

In the sour grapes
Fall of the fittest goes on and on
It doesn't wait
Time moves on and on
It doesn't wait. 2(19)

An ant defeats an elephant
And a rabbit defeats a lion
Weak defeats the fittest
In the final test
Victory of the weakest, goes on and on
It doesn't stop
Time moves on and on
It doesn't wait. 2(20)

Rani of Jhansi fought British
For freedom and for pride
She showed the entire world
Feminine power and its might
Liberation from oppression goes on and on
It doesn't wait
Time moves on and on
It doesn't wait. 2(21)

When even Ram becomes complacent
Ravanas have their day
They show their might and power
Making the weak their prey
As Ravana kills others
And also has his say
Then there is no check
On the Ravana's way

When Ram gets awakened
With a lot of delay
In fight with the Ravana
Ravana gets slayed
Time's slaying goes on and on
It doesn't wait
Time moves on and on
It doesn't wait. 2(22)

Behind the bad actions
There is always malice
Intentions are malafide
So says the Alice
In the woundedland, malice always rules
It tends to follow its own rules
Even the time gets wounded
It also feels hounded
But time provides the healing
Through its hearty feelings
Time moves on and on
It doesn't wait. 2(23)

Whenever there is disorder
Time arrives to set new order
This happens in time and space
In history we see its many trace
Time comes in Krishna's face
To spread his message and his grace
Krishna arrives again and again
To relieve humanity from its pain
Time moves on and on
It doesn't wait. 2(24)

Nature shows its variations
Conditions create new situations
There is an inner quest
In survival of the uniquest
This quest goes on and on
It doesn't wait
Time moves on and on
It doesn't wait. 2(25)

As time becomes material
It reveals its dialectics
Conditions become real
To change the economics and politics
Time's dialectics goes on and on
It doesn't wait
Time moves on and on
It doesn't wait. 2(26)

There is fall of empire
As isms are put to fire
Russia crumbled with communism
Creating new forms of schism
Isms come and go
With the time's flow
Time moves on and on
It doesn't wait. 2(27)

When power shows its oppression
Through its techniques of suppression
Time sends a saviour
To give us freedom and liberation
Saviour comes again and again

On the time's call
Time moves on and on
Giving its own calls
Time moves on and on
It doesn't wait. 2(28)

Truth is crucified
Many many times
Time witnesses it
At the same time
From crucification
A realisation emerges
Enlightening the world
About the wrong surges
Still crucification goes on and on
It doesn't stop
Time moves on and on
It doesn't wait. 2(29)

Modernity launches its invasion
Forests disappear
Life becomes cheap
Commodities become dear
There is a new awakening
Of values and traditions
Traditions go on and on
They don't wait
Time moves on and on
It doesn't wait. 2(30)

Kraunch birds in love play
Were hit by hunter's arrow
Then arose deep pain
In Ramayana it found its flow
Modern hunters destroy nature
Through their polluted bows
They kill many life forms
By their poisonous arrows
Humanity's pain flows on and on
It doesn't stop
Time moves on and on
It doesn't wait. 2(31)

Caste, class and ethnic conflicts
Create in society many rifts
Mahatamas arrive on the scene
To create a harmonic scene
Mahatamas come again and again
They don't stop
Time moves on and on
It doesn't wait. 2(32)

Now time comes to us
And knocks at our door
We welcome it
For new things in store
Time's knocking goes on and on
It doesn't stop
Time moves on and on
And continues to flow. 2(33)

As we bury time capsule
Time refuses to follow the rules
Capsule then remains hidden in the pit
While time continues its skit
Time's motion goes on and on
It doesn't stop
Time moves on and on
It doesn't wait. 2(34)

We are hurt by time's dart
It pierces through our heart
There are many broken parts
We combine them for a new start
New constructions go on and on
They don't stop
Time moves on and on
It doesn't wait. 2(35)

Events happened yesterday
Take a new form
They repeat themselves
In the society and dorms
Events move on and on
They don't stop
Time moves on and on
It doesn't wait. 2(36)

Crisis come and goes
Giving their own blows
As the time's wheel turns
Shadows go for a run

Battles are fought
And wars are won
Time moves on and on
It doesn't wait. 2(37)

Obstructions come in our way
And time slips away
We want to have our say
And time shows its sway
Time's play goes on and on
It doesn't wait
Time moves on and on
It doesn't wait. 2(38)

A chain of events happen
Through the thought weapon
Then cause effect fails
And event rail derails
Time's train moves on and on
It doesn't wait
Time moves on and on
It doesn't wait. 2(39)

Events happen and recede
At their own speed
Many people see
And make their decision trees
Time moves on and on
At its own speed
Time moves on and on
It doesn't wait. 2(40)

Events get blown up
And assume many new shapes
Then they affect everyone
And engulf them in its waves
Time's engulfing goes on and on
It doesn't stop
Time moves on and on
It doesn't wait. 2(41)

When we get caught, in the space-time knot
Then we get reduced, to a mere dot
From the knot as we emerge
We experience a new surge
Our march goes on and on
It doesn't stop
Time moves on and on
It doesn't wait. 2(42)

Consequences of our actions
With time lag they follow
We want to make new corrections
From the experience of high and low
Sooner or later we pay for it
Karma's drama continues its skit
Time's drama goes on and on
It doesn't stop
Time moves on and on
It doesn't wait. 2(43)

As we look into the watch
Time watches us
We move ahead on new paths

Taking Lahore's bus
Time's bus moves on and on
It doesn't stop
Time moves on and on
It doesn't wait. 2(44)

Moments become momentous
Bringing a change in status
Events display their vents
Through the uncertain dents
Like rivers they make new course
And create new history through a new force
Moments move on and on
They don't wait
Time moves on and on
It doesn't wait. 2(45)

We are driving on space-time road
But our mind is somewhere else
We lose the concentration
And experience a sudden stress
A reflex brings us back
To the right track
Our driving goes on and on
It doesn't stop
Time moves on and on
It doesn't wait. 2(46)

Many events happen
To tie us to time's bed
As we take rest
Time moves ahead

On the bed, we think of time
Its arrow's motion and directions
We explore life's events
And their many dimensions
Time's rest and movements go on and on
They don't stop
Time moves on and on
It doesn't wait. 2(47)

As we pass through tribulations
Time provides the healing
Time becomes the medicine
That uplifts our feeling
With the time we recover
As time provides its cover
This recovery goes on and on
It doesn't stop
Time moves on and on
It doesn't wait. 2(48)

Space-time shawl provides shelter
From time's trials and tides
It gives us a new vector
For us to make new strides
New vectors move on and on
They don't wait
Time moves on and on
It doesn't wait. 2(49)

Time reveals the enemies
Time reveals the friends
Time reveals you and me

It reveals new trends
This revelation goes on and on
It doesn't stop
Time moves on and on
It doesn't wait. 2(50)

Time offers us favours
And time devours us
Time spreads its flavours
Time creates the stir
Time's stirring goes on and on
It doesn't stop
Time moves on and on
It doesn't wait. 2(51)

Time's play is unique
It displays its own mystique
When vice and virtue fight
Time reveals its might
Virtue finally wins
Over the deeds of sin
This time's play goes on and on
It doesn't stop
Time moves on and on
It doesn't wait. 2(52)

Now time becomes valentine
Love and joy reveal their shine
Love threads become super fine
Music comes from the shrines

This music flows on and on
It doesn't stop
Time moves on and on
It doesn't wait. 2(53)

Time's arrow and Cupid's arrow
In love there is joy and sorrow
Time lanes are very narrow
Don't wait for tomorrow
Love's arrows move on and on
They don't stop
Time moves on and on
It doesn't wait. 2(54)

Time and tide make a strike
On the life's shore
We witness rise and fall
And make the winning score
Tides come and go
They don't wait
Time moves on and on
It doesn't wait. 2(55)

You take bath in the river Saryu
And witness time passing by you
As we take holy dips
There are no slips
Holy dips go on and on
They don't stop
Time moves on and on
It doesn't wait. 2(56)

From a seed a plant emerges
Plant becomes a tree
Time keeps its count
As zero, one, two and three
Plant creates new seeds
Seeds create new plants
Life goes on and on
It doesn't wait
Time moves on and on
It doesn't wait. 2(57)

Time shows its might
In the conflicts and fights
It gives a new insight
To know who is on the right
Fights go on and on
They don't stop
Time moves on and on
It doesn't wait. 2(58)

We leave behind an image
And come to a new stage
We play a new act
To make a new impact
Images go on and on
They don't wait
Time moves on and on
It doesn't wait. 2(59)

We jump into swimming pool
Waves get generated
They traverse to the other end

With other waves they get nested
Time's nesting goes on and on
It doesn't stop
Time moves on and on
It doesn't wait. 2(60)

On the freeway you slow down
From behind traffic could knock you down
You learn to drive on life's freeway
Moving along with time's ray
This learning goes on and on
It doesn't stop
Time moves on and on
It doesn't wait. 2(61)

As and when you jump a signal
Cop imposes fine
He yells on you with his might
To make you fall in line
Time's signal goes on and on
It doesn't stop
Time moves on and on
It doesn't wait. 2(62)

With each step we gain confidence
To take the next step
Step by step we move ahead
And fill the new gap
Time's steps go on and on
They don't wait
Time moves on and on
It doesn't wait. 2(63)

As we solve a tricky problem
New problems come
Problems then multiply
Through new puzzles and sums
Problems go on and on
They don't stop
Time moves on and on
It doesn't wait. 2(64)

When time spreads its grace
We see it on person's face
There is no need to chase
Maya's mirage with a craze
Time's grace comes on and on
It doesn't wait
Time moves on and on
It doesn't wait. 2(65)

Space-time and the circus net
Share similar features
As we jump down on the nets
We jump up by their curvatures
Time's jumping goes on and on
It doesn't stop
Time moves on and on
It doesn't wait. 2(66)

Time flies on its wings
Creating many stirrings
With past and future as its wings
Present does the running

Bird of time flies on and on
It doesn't stop
Time moves on and on
It doesn't wait. 2(67)

As we pass the day
Day becomes past
Night comes as future
And future moves fast
Between the day and light
There is twilight
Between past and future
Present shows its might
Present's show goes on and on
It doesn't stop
Time moves on and on
It doesn't wait. 2(68)

There is twist of fate
In the time's slate
Making us reach early
Or delaying us to get late
Twists of fate go on and on
It doesn't wait
Time moves on and on
It doesn't wait. 2(69)

There are many events
That become part of frozen moments
Moments slowly die
Making us laugh and cry

Events move on and on
They don't wait
Time moves on and on
It doesn't wait. 2(70)

We move on time's track
On events we look back
They pale into insignificance
As we move into future tense
Time's track moves on and on
It doesn't wait
Time moves on and on
It doesn't wait. 2(71)

Time shows its manifestation
In the rhythms of nature
We feel its vibration
In the self and other creatures
Nature's rhythms move on and on
It doesn't wait
Time moves on and on
It doesn't wait. 2(72)

Part III

Religious Arrow of Time

Vishnu Came As Mohini
3(1) - 3(28)

Arrow of Time

(III)

Echoes from the future
Come to us as a voice
Taking our care
And informing us the choice
The echoes come on and on
They don't wait
Time moves on and on
It doesn't wait. 3(1)

Tree emerges from the seed
Hidden in a lump
We take a few steps
And then take a quantum jump
Limits show their limit
In the nature's skit
But we break the limits
By our own writ
Limits crossings go on and on
It doesn't stop
Time moves on and on
It doesn't wait. 3(2)

In the garden of Eden
Snake continues its enticing
We long for the last temptation
To eat the apple that is shining
Temptations go on and on
They don't stop
Time moves on and on
It doesn't wait. 3(3)

For every positive number
There is an opposite number
Numbers create actions
With equal and opposite reactions
The number game goes on and on
It doesn't wait
Time moves on and on
It doesn't wait. 3(4)

Bhasmasur made Shiva running
Vishnu came as Mohini
Luring him to dancing
Saved Shiva from tyranny
Liberation goes on and on
As the time intervenes
Time moves on and on
It doesn't wait. 3(5)

We hear voices from the time's cave
Har Har Mahadev, Har Har Mahadev
These voices are repeated billion times
In America and Haridwar at the same time

Time's reverberations go on and on
They don't stop
Time moves on and on
It doesn't wait. 3(6)

As we see through time's spectacle
We then see many miracles
Arrow hits Ravana's navel
Voices come from Tower of Babel
There is execution and resurrection
Life's train again moves on traction
Resurrections go on and on
It doesn't wait
Time moves on and on
It doesn't wait. 3(7)

Gods and demons bow to time
Time shows them the way
Defeat and victory is matter of time
In time's unique play
There are circles within circles
In the time's cycle
Time's cycle moves on and on
It doesn't wait
Time moves on and on
It doesn't wait. 3(8)

Abhimanyu gets entangled
In time's chakravyuh
He fights to the end
Without knowing the last cue

He remains immortal
Others become mortal
Abhimanyu fights on and on
He doesn't stop
Time moves on and on
It doesn't wait. 3(9)

When it is our time
Yama comes in time
Only Savitri can make
Even Yama very kind
There is end of our history
But time doesn't end
Time moves on and on
It doesn't wait. 3(10)

Satyuga, Dwapar, Treta and Kaliyuga
They all hang on time's hook
As pages turn on time's book
They show their faces and the look
Social pages turn on and on
With the time's hand
Time moves on and on
It doesn't wait. 3(11)

Every action has its reflection
In the parallel universe
Reflections get accumulated
Bringing us boon or curse
Our karmas go on and on
It doesn't wait

Time moves on and on
It doesn't wait. 3(12)

Time become space and space becomes time
In the space-time yantra they intertwine
When Shiva manifests as space and Shakti as time
In their union, space-time shows its shine
Space time union goes on and on
It doesn't stop
Time moves on and on
It doesn't wait. 3(13)

On the space-time fabric
There are many knots
All historical events
Are printed on it as dots
These dots are very fascinating
As to them we are relating
Dots add on and on
As history moves on
Time moves on and on
It doesn't wait. 3(14)

Space and time get frozen
In various cosmic zones
Waiting for Rama's arrival
For his touch of the stone
Ahilaya comes alive
To move on and on
Time moves on and on
It doesn't wait. 3(15)

The arrow hits Krishna's toe
And continues to flow
Arjuna gets defeated
Merely by a bow
This arrow shows its power
In seconds of every hour
Time moves on and on
It doesn't wait. 3(16)

Life emerges through God's volition
Through the co-evolution
From co-evolution comes evolution
Through nature's manifestation
Time's manifestation goes on and on
It doesn't stop
Time moves on and on
It doesn't wait. 3(17)

'God is not needed'
To explain many things
So said Darwin
Reducing God to a small thing
God then manifested
In the form of time
Time became a new name
For the God's rhyme
Time's rhymes go on and on
They don't stop
Time moves on and on
It doesn't wait. 3(18)

As Wu-Li masters dance to time
We know the tune of the time
Spin, symmetry and charm's show
Organic energy continues to flow
Masters dance on and on
They don't stop
Time moves on and on
It doesn't wait. 3(19)

Time offers us challenge
To the challenge we respond
Challenge and response create new waves
In the time's pond
Responses move on and on
They don't wait
Time moves on and on
It doesn't wait. 3(20)

Time moves at different velocities
On different planets
We simulate such happenings
On the internet
Planets move on and on
They don't stop
Time moves on and on
It doesn't wait. 3(21)

Time is God and God is Time
This revelation was missed
Even by Einstein
In the holy Gita
We do find

Time is God and God is time
Time's cosmic show goes on and on
It doesn't wait
Time moves on and on
It doesn't wait. 3(22)

Time is truth and truth is time
It reveals itself at the correct time
At the moment of its darshan
Energy flows in tonnes
Energy flows on and on
It doesn't stop
Time moves on and on
It doesn't wait. 3(23)

Brief history of time
Is written on every grain
From big-bang to blackholes
We see it through time's curtain
Curtain raising goes on and on
It doesn't stop
Time moves on and on
It doesn't wait. 3(24)

Even in 'end of physics'
Time provides its kicks
In the end of the end
The arrow shows new bends
Time's arrow moves on and on
It doesn't stop
Time moves on and on
It doesn't wait. 3(25)

Time's arrow started moving
With the big bang
Then time found its expression
In the Yin and Yang
Time's bang goes on and on
It doesn't stop
Time moves on and on
It doesn't wait. 3(26)

Time's poetry is unending
Taking curious turns and bendings
It would continue to move
Without waiting for me and you
Leaving behind its own prints
For the future giving some hints
Time moves on and on
It doesn't wait. 3(27)

From blackholes to nirvana point
Runs the time's arrow
Time's entire spectrum
Many want to know
Leaving behind the blackholes
For the nirvana we go
Time moves on and on
It doesn't wait. 3(28)

Part IV

Spiritual Arrow of Time

Miraculous
4(1) - 4(25)

Arrow of Time

(IV)

4(1) Miraculous
4(2) Adam and Eve
4(3) Circle of Consciousness
4(4) A Point of Light
4(5) Lady With A Lamp
4(6) Space Time Dance
4(7) Temple of Five Goddesses
4(8) Sparkling Light
4(9) Mr. Might and Mr. Right
4(10) War Against Evil
4(11) Step By Step
4(12) Oh Rio
4(13) This World is Very Crazy
4(14) Zero and One
4(15) Kaun tvam: Who Are You?
4(16) Harmony and Harmony
4(17) Law of Karma
4(18) Prism of Ism
4(19) You Are the Mantra
4(20) Divine Driver
4(21) I Will Come Again
4(22) Hari Om Hari

4(23) Hare Krishna Hare Rama
4(24) You are In Every Home
4(25) Learn and Repeat Name of Rama

Miraculous

Scientists are still in a fix
Why nature behaves as a double helix
Matter and energy are connected by a thread
Without Shakti, Shiva is dead.

There are miracles and miracles and miracles
Because this world is miraculous
Miraculous, miraculous
Miraculous, miraculous.

Bus fell in the pit
Every body was fit, Miraculous...
Train met an accident
There was no dent, Miraculous...

There was a bomb blast
Your friend was fine at last, Miraculous...
There was a terrorist
No scratch even on the wrist, Miraculous...

There was a hijack
Plane landed on the track, Miraculous
A man fell from Tipu point
No hurt even on joints, Miraculous...

A man was near death
And regained the last breath, Miraculous...
There was a resurrection
Man came back in action, Miraculous...
Man came out of the grave
Started doing his own shave, Miraculous... 1(1)

Adam and Eve

Adam is body and Eve is soul
They were unitd as a whole.

In the garden of Eden
There was perfection
Snakes of vices
Offered the seduction.

Snake then tempted Adam and Eve
Listen to me, listen to my brief
Come and taste the beautiful apple
Just taste it as a sample.

Soul's intellect was then coloured
Its vision was also little blurred
Eve told Adam let's taste the apple
In the garden of Eden, things are in ample.

Thus then began their original sin
They were separated from the heavenly inn
Body and soul then felt the alienation
As a result of first temptation.

Soul cried to return to the original state
But body kept enjoying the material fate
Since that separation the two are crying
Though for a union they are trying.

In a unique place I found them in union
In a blissful state and "holi" communion. 4(2)

Circle of Consciousness

Standing near the sea
I was enjoying the cool breeze
Uncountable waves
Touching the shore
They were also reaching
My heart's core.

Waves after waves
Were hitting the rock
Rock stood firm
To take the stock
There was no need
For any clock
Time became the key
To open space time lock.

From the thought ocean
Many waves arise
Continuing their journey
Through fall and rise
Circle of consciousness
Then expands
Encircling the entire
Cosmic land.

Suddenly
I was reminded
Of Vivekananda rock memorial
Sending spiritual waves

That are real
Whenever humanity
Will be losing its patience
This rock would continue
To spread spiritual radiance. 4(3)

A Point of Light

At Abu
Academy for Better Universe
I heard nature's new verse.

At the sunset point
In wonder people walk
To the setting sun
They ask
What is your purpose
What is your task.

Sun says, I am coming again
To spread my radiance
And bring the rains.

Beyond these universes
There is another sun
Which neither sets nor burns
It is a bright point of light
Illuminating the universe with its sight
It simply sends its divine rays
To guide humanity
And mould its ways.

Its rays provide the rays of hope
Continue your journey don't stop
Continue your journey don't stop
Don't stop, don't stop
Continue your journey, don't stop. 4(4)

Lady With A Lamp

In complete darkness
There was need for brightness
The lady moved around in search of lamp
To increase the brightness with many amps.

As she lighted it
The room was completely lit
There was glow on her face
Which radiated the time and space.

Lighting the lamp was ecstatic
The event created its own magic
I was witnessing truth, goodness and beauty
As the space and time were filled with tranquillity.

With the flow of cool breeze
It was a moment of bliss, joy and peace
Space became dynamic and moment static
Every one's heart became very poetic.

The moment of lady lighting the lamp
Left behind a permanent stamp
There was sudden glow of hope
I heard some rhythms of the 'quantum rope'.

I was wondering all the time
Why was this moment appearing so prime
Was it a moment of poetic illusion
Or it was beginning of a new creation. 4(5)

Space Time Dance

Moon still clouds moving
Clouds still moon is moving
Moon and cloud both are moving
Or is it that my heart is moving.

Full moon behind the clouds
Emerging from the shadow of shroud
Brightness followed by darkness
Spreading radiance and the coolness.

Teaching us a lesson of life
Darkness is a passing side
Beyond the shadow of events
There lies the divine current.

Time is static it doesn't move
Space curves in various hoves
Time and space dance together
With the sounds that live for ever.

Once in a blue moon
There is a grand spectacle
Arising in us a curiosity
And wonder at life's miracle. 4(6)

Temple of Five Goddesses

Trees moving, leaves fluttering
Birds singing, peacocks dancing
Humans moving, plants sprouting
All these simply uplift my feeling.

Wells empty, some semi-full
Life has a meaning, it is completely full
Life is moving at a smooth pace
No need for running any race.

At the temple of five Godesses
People leave behind their addresses
For the happiness of all people
For their wishes to be fulfilled.

Nice people, pious people
You don't feel at all crippled
They make you feel completely fine
They appear almost divine.

4(7)

Sparkling Light

Dark night lonely road
Stars twinkling with a great show
I become part of a different mode
As I listen to nature's ode.

Banyan tree shows its majesty
Hundreds of fireflies move in modesty
Dancing to the tune of tranquillity
I witness truth, love and beauty.

Old and new coexist
Both manifesting their geist
Showing us their respective strengths
By complementing each other's dent.

There is a lesson for the humans
To spark like the firefly
And give light to others
In their own rhythmic style. 4(8)

Mr. Might and Mr. Right

All the time people say
Satyemev jayate, satyemev jayate.

Arjuna knows how to fight
Krishna tells what is right
Evil always shows its might
But good has the foresight.

Good may experience a big crash
As evil tries to reduce it to trash
Good then arises from the ash
To give the evil the final smash
Smash then turns into a victory
This drama becomes part of history.

Conflict between the good and evil
Fight between the Gods and devils
This story is repeated in space and time
And is told to the masses from temples and shrines.

Listening this people say
Satyemev jayate, Satyemev Jayate

Those who have the final faith
Know that Mr. Right will prevail
In the fight between might and right
Right always brings the light.

Once again people say
Satyamev jayate, Satyemev Jayate. 4(9)

War Against Evil

When war against evil is a continuing war
Liberation from oppression is not very far.

Rama fought Ravana in a war
Because war against evil is a continuing war
Pandavas fought the great Mahabharat war
Because war against evil is a continuing war.

Jesus body wore a number of scars
Because war against evil is a continuing war
Gandhi fought for liberation through non-violent war
Because war against evil is a continuing war.

When war against evil is a continuing war
Liberation from oppression is not very far. 4(10)

Step by Step

Step by step
And step by step.

We climb the mountain
Step by step
Step by step and step by step.

We go to the moon
And take a new step
Step by step and step by step.

We make a quantum jump
And take a new step
Step by step and step by step.

We achieve the success
And move ahead
Step by step and step by step.

We take a new jump
And move ahead
Step by step and step by step.

We move ahead
We move ahead
Step by step and step by step
Step by step and step by step. 4(11)

Oh Rio

Oh Rio Oh Rio
I love your scenario.

I look through the windows
I see the meadows
I feel the wind's flow
Oh Rio...

I listen to the sounds
In nature that abounds
I feel the nice echo
Oh Rio...

I look at the tree
I want to float free
And fly like the sparrow
Oh Rio...

I listen to the rhymes
In the space and in time
Tide is high and low
Oh Rio...

I walk through the jungles
And cross the rivers
Cranes fly in a row
Oh Rio...

I move through the Bungalow
I see a temple
Inside the rainbow
Oh Rio...

I pay my salaam
I say Ram Ram
I lift the Rama's bow
Oh Rio...

I love carnival
You are musical
I hear the fall of snow
Oh Rio...

Oh Rio Oh Rio
I love your scenario. 4(12)

This World is Very Crazy

This world is very crazy
This world is very crazy.

Kathak becomes very zazzy
Events become very mazy
This world...

Things turn topsy turvy
Dances become very curvy
This world...

Computers turn very fuzzy
Hackers become very crazy
This world...

Idli dosa gravy
No need for any levy
This world...

Some are simply lazy
Some become vey crazy
This world...

Sanskrit Hindi Angreji
This world is very crazy

No right choice O baby
This world is very crazy
This world is very crazy.

4(13)

Zero and One

You are zero I am one
We are the cause of this creation
I am zero you are one
We are the cause of this creation.

Zero and the one get all the things done
We are the cause of this creation.

Small smaller smallest
Big bigger biggest
Which one is the best
Which one is the best
You don't know and I don't know
We are the cause of this creation.

What is beyond the zero and the one
Who has the answer to this question
You don't know and I don't know
We are the cause of this creation.

Zero and the one make binary system
Making computers go for run
You are zero I am one
We are the cause of this creation. 4(14)

Kaun-tvam: Who Are You?

Who are you, who are you?
Who are you, who are you?

An engineer, a teacher
An architect or proctor
A philosopher or professor
An executive or executioner
Who are you...

A capitalist or communist
God fearing or atheist
A liberal or fundamentalist
Conformist or reformist
Revolutionary or reactionary
Who are you...

A doctor or curator
A lawyer or a liar
A merchant or an exploiter
A worker or a fighter
Who are you...

An economist or a social scientist
Ready to make the data twist
A hippie or a yuppie
Unable to take care of one's puppy
Who are you... 4(15)

Harmony and Harmony

Harmony and harmony
Say harmony and harmony.

Harmony with nature
Harmony with creature
Harmony with mind
And harmony with matter
Harmony...

Harmony in relations
And harmony with nations
Harmony with thought
And harmony with action
Harmony...

Harmony with self
And harmony with others
Harmony with present
And harmony with future
Harmony...

Harmony with science
And harmony with conscience
Harmony in chaos
And harmony with cosmos
Harmony... 4(16)

Law of Karma

Crucification and resurrection
Law of karma is in operation.

New creations and destruction
Law of karma...

Hate and jealousy
Love and affection
Law of karma...

Thought and actions have interconnections
Law of karma...

Sacrifices and the passions
Law of karma...

You pay the price for bad actions
Law of karma...

Action reaction and counter action
Law of karma...

Krishna takes new incarnations
Law of karma... 4(17)

Prism of ism

Ism, ism, ism, ism
We see the world through many prism
I get the rhythm of a nazm
As I see the world through many prism.

Socialism, Marxism
We see...

Racism, Terrorism
We see...

Militarism, Capitalism
We see...

Consumerism, Egoism
We see...

Idealism, Realism
We see...

Secularism, Atheism
We see...

Feminism, Humanism
We see...

Jainism, Buddhism
We see...

Sikhism, Shintoism
We see...

Gandhism, Romanticism
We see...

Mysticism, Hinduism
We see...

Materialism, Spiritualism
We see... 4(18)

You are the Mantra

You are the sound, you are the mantra
You are the yantra, you are the tantra.

You are the Shakti, you are the Bhakti
You are the Riddhi, you are the Siddhi
You are the sound...

You are the light, you are the sight
You are the day and you are the night
You are the sound...

You are the music, you are the raga
You are the way and you are the marga
You are the sound...

You are love and you are compassion
You are the truth and its perfection
You are the sound...

You are beauty and you are goodness
You are the bliss and you are the godess
You are the sound... 4(19)

Divine Driver

You create particles and anti-particles
You are creator of all the articles.

You are remover of all obstacles
You are maker of all miracles
You are controller of life cycle
You are present in the void and the null
You create particles...

We can't see but you see us
Whether we are alone or we are in rush
You are creator of divine force field
Always providing us protective shield
You create particles...

When we move into the future
You act as our torch bearer
We remember you at every hour
You bestow on us your divine shower
You create particles...

You can reverse the arrow of time
Making broken pieces combine
You operate through many dimensions
We are longing for your darshan
You create particles...

You create material things from nothing
We always beg for your blessings
You are always our great protector
In your feet we take shelter
You create particles...

You are driver of life's vehicle
Taking us beyond life death cycle
You take us from hell to heaven
In the end making all accounts even
You create particles... 4(20)

I Will Come Again

I will come again, I will come again
I will come again to remove humanity's pain.

Whenever there is disorder
I come down to set new order
I come again and again
To bring the needed change.

Whenever there is decline
I come to make things fine
I come again and again
To bring the needed change.

When vice-virtue see saw
Gets out of balance
I then come again
To bring the needed change.

Those who have the faith
Know that I will come again
I will come again
To bring the needed change. 4(21)

Hari Om Hari

Hari Om Hari
Hari Om Hari
When God is with you
You don't worry.

Shiva took the poison
That arose from the churning
He removed the worries
That were continuously burning
Hari Om Hari...
God's help comes
Like Draupadi's sari
Countering Duryodhana's
Attempt at injury
Hari Om Hari...

All the might
Went to Kaurava's side
As Krishna's help came
Pandavas didn't worry
Hari Om Hari...

Jesus died on the cross
To take our worries
Hari Om Hari... 4(22)

Hare Krishna Hare Rama

Hare Krishna Hare Rama....

Have a drink of karma cola
Hola hola hola hola
Moksha dhrama artha kama
Hare Krishna Hare Rama.

Have perfection through the karma
By performing your swadharma
Alpha beta sigma gama
Hare Krishna Hare Rama.

Tune into your atma
Listen straight to parmatma
This is life's terra firma
Hare Krishna Hare Rama.

You are full of love and devotion
You are the light of new generation
Life is always full of drama
Hare Krishna Hare Rama.

You are the hope of human liberation
You are the call of futurization
You always show your charisma
Hare Krishna Hare Rama. 4(23)

You Are In Every Home

You are in every home
We say Hari Om
O Rabba, O Rabba.

You are in Dwaba
You are in Dacca
O Rabba...

You are in Jerusalam
You belong to every dharam
O Rabba...

You are in Rome
Hari Om Hari Om
O Rabba ...

You are in Dwarika
You are in America
O Rabba...

You are the bliss and peace
You increase our life's lease
O Rabba...

You are the final goal
Filling goodness in our soul
O Rabba...

You are the final light
Making us feel bright
O Rabba...

You are in every home
We say Om Om
O Rabba... 4(24)

Learn and Repeat Name of Rama

Pleasure, pain, sin and merit
Saint, sinner and day and night
Rise and fall, up and down
Losing wearing of the crown
Learn and repeat name of Rama
Rise above and see the drama. 4(25-1)

High and low, gods and demons
Action reaction, fission and fusion
Wealth poverty nector poison
Maya is this world's illusion
Learn and repeat.... 4(25-2)

Heaven, hell, rich and poor
Good, evil, saviour and butcher
There are many pairs of opposite
Which are part of nature's deposits
Learn and repeat... 4(25-3)

Verb, adjective, noun, pronoun
They are merely maya's sound
Space and time intertwine
Maya shows its various signs
Learn and repeat... 4(25-4)

With the wind dust also rises
Throwing mud creates the crises
Men of judgement make distinction
What is good and bad in action
Learn and repeat... 4(25-5)

Life and death, length and breadth
Body mind spirit and breath
They are miracles of creation
Of space-time and causation
Learn and repeat.... 4(25-6)

Revolution, evolution and involution
Position, opposition and proposition
Friendship, enemity show their relation
Envy, jealousy affect the situation
Learn and repeat.... 4(25-7)

Lust, anger, vanity and the greed
To the hell they all lead
Persons then fall with a speed
As a result of their own deeds
Learn and repeat... 4(25-8)

Effect of karma, time or nature
Make even good lose their stature
But good always comes up again and again
To bring the happiness and the joyous rain
Learn and repeat... 4(25-9)

Kalnemi, Ravana and Rahu
They all live here and now
Ruling with power and might
Making fearful day and night
Learn and repeat... 4(25-10)

Though wicked may also do good deeds
Wickedness is inherent in this creed
Because of power they may succeed

To their might this world may yield
Learn and repeat... 4(25·11)

To sound advice wicked don't heed
They are fuelled with power need
When the epic ends, people read
Wickeds are exposed and virtue leads
Learn and repeat... 4(25-12)

When evil forces get defeated
That moment gets celebrated
There is joy everywhere
As nature's justice is very fair
Learn and repeat... 4(25-13)

Rebellions, revolutions and revelations
In many forms they make manifestation
People wait for a new incarnation
To uplift the face of human relations
Learn and repeat... 4(25-14)

Space and time create a warp for you
About which you have no clue
You traverse on paths old and new
From the previous birth some accounts are due
Learn and repeat... 4(25-15)

Human greed creates many forces
Leading to drying up of resources
Rivers are forced to change their courses
Indices go up and down in bourses
Learn and repeat... 4(25-16)

Light is generated from the oil and wick
Nature shows its dialectics

History, psychology, economics and politics
Where are values where are ethics
Learn and repeat... 4(25-17)

Nature operates through natural selection
In many forms we see its manifestation
Some prefer the self-selection
To lead society for an upwards motion
Learn and repeat... 4(25-18)

Satyuga, dwapar, treta and kaliyuga
Through them time shows its many looks
Values are taught through the holy books
To change the world and its outlook
Learn and repeat... 4(25-19)

Truth, goodness and beauty
Liberty, equality and fraternity
Roam with freedom in cosmic city
Showing compassion, empathy and peity
Learn and repeat.... 4(25-19)

Pleasure, pain, sin and merit
Saint sinner and day and night
Rise and fall up and down
Losing wearing of the crown
Learn and repeat name of Rama
Rise above and see the drama. 4(25-20)

Inspirational Sources

This work has been influenced by a number of inspirational sources that include spiritual and scientific books, interactions with a large number of individuals belonging to various strata of society, interactions with friends across the globe, family interactions etc. Creativity triggers also emanated from visits to various places within the country and abroad. While it is impossible to list all the sources of influence, in particular, following books have been sources of inspiration in varying forms:

- *A Brief History of Time: From the Big Bang to the Blackholes*, W Stephen Hawking, Bantam Books, New York, 1988.
- *Autobiography of a Yogi*, Paramahansa Yogananda, Self-Realization Fellowship, Los Angeles, 1948.
- *Fabric of the Universe*, Denis Postle, Macmillan, London, 1976.
- *Holistic Science and Vedanta*, Swami Jitatmananda, Bhartiya Vidhya Bhavan, Bombay, 1991.
- *India by Al-biruni,* Queyamuddin Ahmad, National Book Trust, New Delhi, 1983.
- *Modern Physics and Vedanta,* Swami Jitatmananda, Bhartiya Vidhya Bhavan, Bombay, 1992.

- *Mysticism and the New Physics,* Michael Talbot, Bantam Books, New York, 1981.
- *Philosophy at War with Positivism,* Borana Bebek, Routledge & Kegan Paul, London, 1982.
- *Rishi Vision,* Swami Bodhananda, Sambodh Foundation, New Delhi, 1992.
- *Science and Mysticism: The Essence of Vedic Philosophy,* H.K.Kesavan, New Age International Publishers, New Delhi, 1997.
- *Structure of Scientific Revolutions,* Thomas Kuhn, University of Chicago Press, Chicago, 1962.
- *The Arrow of Time: The Quest to Solve Science's Greatest Mystery,* Peter Coveney and Roger Highfield, Flamingo, London, 1991.
- *The Bhagvad Gita,* Swami Chidbahvananda, Sri Rama Krishna Tapovan, Tirupparaitturai, 1988.
- *The Dancing Wu Li Masters,* Gary Zukav, Marrow Hill, New York, 1979.
- *The Everything and the Nothing,* Meher Baba, Meher House Publications, Bombay, 1963.
- *The River of Time*, Igor D.Novikov, Cambridge University Press, 1998.
- *The Tao of Physics,* Fritjof Capra, Bantam Books, Toronto, 1976.
- *The Turning Point,* Fritjof Capra, Simon and Schuster, New York, 1992.
- *The Science of Spirituality*, M.K.Kaw, Full Circle Publishing, New Delhi, 2000.

- *Taoism: The Way of the Mystic*, J.C.Cooper, Acquarian Press, Kent, 1990.
- *Quantum Questions,* Ken Wilber, Shambala, New York, 1984.
- *Vachananjali: A Prayer book*, Mahaswamiji Shivacharya Shivamurty, Sri Taralbalu Jagadguru, Sringeri, 1994.
- *Visions: How Science will Revolutionize the 21st Century & Beyond,* Michio Kaku, Oxford University Press, Oxford, 1998.

Management in New Age: Western Windows Eastern Doors, Subhash Sharma

New Age International (P) Ltd., Publishers, New Delhi (1996)

'Those in the field of management education can find quite a few exciting, non-traditional and revolutionary points of view'

—*Business Standard*

'Anyone interested in indigenous matter on organizational behaviour must go through this book'

—*The Hindu*

'Dr. Sharma's book is full of gems'

— *Maharashtra Herald*

'Well written and thought provoking'

—*Journal of Human Values*

'Dr. Sharma writes with a clarity and directness that should make sense to any student of management, Western or Eastern'

—*Chinmaya Management Review*

'We recommend this book for the senior executives and management teachers. This will give them an insight and make their mental horizon broader'

—*Vivek Management*

'Book should particularly appeal to a Western mind wanting to know more about Indianism. To an Indian student, the book should be an eye opener'

—*Productivity*

'The book is a path-breaking venture in the realm of management'

—*Administrative Change*

'An elixir for mind liberation'

Analyst

Quantum Rope: Science, Mysticism & Management,
Subhash Sharma
New Age International (P) Ltd., Publishers,
New Delhi (1999)

For those who thought science is highbrow stuff full of black and white facts, this book adds some colour by exploring new terrain of mysticism... Go through the pages and find out.

—*Science Express*

It is not just any book on science or mysticism. Author takes pains to prove that Science and Mysticism are the two banks of a river connected by the 'Quantum rope' which is the bridge... The Sanskritized interpretation of English scientific terms are interesting indeed.

—*The Statesman Literary Supplement*

This book should be a welcome addition to any thinking man's library.

—*The New Indian Express*

The author is well known for his provocative, eye-opener, and revolutionary ideas. His ideas are stimulating. His experiments in presenting the concepts are unique... Readers can enjoy his book in a relaxed mood while travelling and at the same time researchers and pundits can get turnaround ideas for their thesis.

—*Vivek Management*

The book is unique in that the relationship between science, mysticism and management has been through the medium of poetic expressions i.e. verses... The author deserves congratulations for bringing out an unusual book on management.

- *Abhigyan*

The author has nicely presented an assimilation of paradigms and theories of science with viewpoints of mysticism... It provides a framework to the readers to think in new directions in innovative ways.

—Management & Change

Dr. Sharma's book is valuable not only for the rich imagery employed to develop a new paradigm but also for the ideas it generates in reader's mind. Serious students would find it a source of inspiration for embarking on their own brands of 'lateral thinking' in management techniques.

—IIMB Management Review

'Quantum Rope' is an unusual book of scientific verses combined with notes on the verses and short essays.

—Sankalpa

Creation from Shunya

Published by Deepak Joshi, Bombay (1993)

It was sheer joy reading the wonderful book of poems, `Cretation from Shunya'. Dr. Sharma has touched deftly the core of Indian philosophy, its intrinsic essence, spiritual grandeur and the mystic aura. In simplest lines he has painted the pictures of sublimity glorifying the sacred concept of shunya.

—Dr. Dwarakanath H Kabadi

Founder-President, Poets International Organization
Bangalore

Creation from Shunya', is really fantastic. I liked, Why run the race?, House of Demand and Supply, Models of man, Science is microscopic, OM: Original Mantra and other poems. The ideas in the book are so refreshing.

—Swami Someshwarananda

Chairman, Vivekananda Centre for Indian Management
Indore